the Wrath of Kali

Michael D. Nordhart

Song of the Rushes

Omaha, Nebraska

Paperback: 978-1-7375721-5-2
Kindle: 978-1-7375721-6-9

Cataloging-in-Publication Data on file with the publisher.

Printed and bound in the United States of America
10 9 8 7 6 5 4 3

❧

"The master is a child, a fool, a man asleep,

a leaf tumbling in the wind."

"We glimpse his nature only through paradox."

Thomas Byrom

More Notes from the Playground

He placed an antique children's lunch box onto the plank seat of the picnic table and while still holding his large drawing tablet, sat down, facing outward, relaxed his muscles and leaned his back onto the edge of the tabletop. The drawing tablet, that lay on his lap, waited for his meditation to choose for him the scene he would reflect. The lunch box contained a sandwich (he preferred cheese, cheddar, no mayonnaise, because it could keep longer), a small thermos of strong black coffee, a portion of potato chips for contrast to the cheese sandwich, and a piece of chocolate. In the right-side pocket of his jacket, extra drawing pencils, erasers, a slim box containing some wax-based crayons. He had recently acquired a set of pastels, though he rarely attempted painting, even with minimal abstraction.

As the layers of theme are for a musician, so are the wave lengths of color to a serious artist. He dare not embarrass himself by attempting to reflect those—not quite yet. In black and white he was well practiced. Three eraser tipped pencils of soft, medium, and hard graphite were in his breast pocket, along with his reading glasses. These he did not wear while sketching. Their lenses and rims got in the way of his depth perception. They were for his paperback copy of an edited "War and Peace", which he kept in the left side pocket of his jacket. He had read the entire novel but kept this little copy with him so that he could open to any random page and enter a room or a battlefield where the familiar characters were acting out a scene, the entire context of which they were not aware, yet innocently beautiful within.

The leaves answering the movement of a breeze inspired him to lean forward and give attention. The brushes of the branches of dark distant trees were casting their dance onto a blue canvas, fluid as a stream's current fluctuating the tiny hairs and feathers of an artfully designed fly on a fisherman's hook. Amused at this metaphor, of himself as a fish being enticed by the touch of something in nature, he breathed in deep and exhaled, anticipating the picture he would be inspired to draw. He waited, still as the tablet, relaxed and ready.

On the far side of an open area, near and almost under those ancient oaks and ash, were a couple picnic tables and some rusty playground equipment: Swing set, little merry-go-round, monkey bars. The scene was far away, but that did not matter, since he could mentally place himself at any point of view; closer, at a distance, and with an intuitive grasp of the three dimensional, draw an object at an angle outside of his physical location and line of sight. This talent was originally discovered, accidentally, when he was a beginner at practicing depth perception. In the examination of a finished sketch, he could see that some of his diminishing lines were not in harmony.

He most certainly was not averse to a painting by a grand master being out of proportion, especially in renaissance religious works, believing that correct perspective (except for the very naïve or lazy artists) was intuitively disregarded in concentration on spiritual theme. There is nothing special about correct perspective that makes it an absolute requirement. Very often, it was not something to be bothered with. Perspective was also purposely manipulated for altar pieces to enhance the other-worldly nuance of scenes, such as the Adoration of the Magi and the Annunciation. In modern painting, the cryptic and abstract quality of the surrealists, (if peaceful, melancholy and inspired by a sense of humor and good intention), offered a pleasant disturbance, like as a child exploring a haunted house. But the Violent molesting of the psyche, obvious or subliminal, by the ill motivated egotistical elitists or the grossly indulgent, he averted his eyes from. The obsessive grotesque was assigned to its metaphysical nightmare alley of sadomasochism. If an artist's work did make it out of the tavern to where a painting or a play was visible in the daylight, he might condescend a look at it and make a judgment.

Otherwise, he would not venture into those narrow back streets to have a conversation or a possible knife fight with a drunken Marlowe or a murderous Caravaggio—even if he did appreciate the bravery of their explorations as depicted in their art. Preferring a gentle atmosphere, he would have enjoyed an association with the Mediterranean sun loving Picasso and the eccentric Erik Satie when the two of them were producing experimental ballets with Debussy in Paris. An afternoon espresso in a sidewalk café would have been allowed. No Absinthe, thank you. He was sure he would have enjoyed their company. Although, he had to admit that he hated most of the paintings by Picasso for the same reason he hated soloist virtuoso violinists who screeched sexual frustrations of some drug addicted spoiled composer. Sibelius, for instance.

If he broke the rules of perspective, he would be considerate of the viewer. In the process of correcting the errors of his first sketches, he developed the ability to place his point of view in any position he liked. This worked well when surreptitiously drawing people. He watched them move about and remembered their basic form. When they sat down in such a way that hid their attributes, if they positioned their body into a dull position, such as in profile, he mentally positioned himself where he imagined he would see more of the person. Glancing briefly at the subject out of the corner of his eye, he would draw from that other point of view.

For the present drawing, he would pretend he was standing only a few feet from the playground. After flipping to the first page of the tablet, he rested his open hand on the blank sheet of paper. He took note of a sliver of sunlight blinking out as the sun moved in relation to a tree nearby. Contemplating the ambiguity of time, he laughed, lightly and silently to himself. Being of meta-physical bent, he would be amused by drifting thoughts. How big is a ray of light? And what is a spot? If it is conceived of as a small point, it might be looked at by more than one person. But if one imagines it to be large and spherical, and if one were inside of it, as like in a flood light, would they be able to see? Blinded, with no reflection, would there be only the sense of darkness? He returned his gaze to the grassy expanse directly in front of him, where couples lounged on blankets, three teen-agers played Frisbee and some children kicked a ball back and forth in their quasi-soccer game. Casually, he wandered his eyes over and beyond the small field of soft-mown grass to the trees on the other side of that open area.

When he brought his attention down from the floating tops of the branches and rested it on the playground, he noticed one child, a girl, nonchalantly walking very slowly around, as if nostalgically examining the playground equipment. Sadly, his adult mind projected. There were no other children. Only her. Too far away for him to physically see her face, he nevertheless settled on her and her environment as the subject. He removed the three pencils and a sharpener from his pocket and placed them on the bench beside him. Taking his time, not at all worried about the model running away, knowing the universe will change and into something interesting regardless of how quickly one may try to take a picture of the sun setting behind the trees, the mist as it floats over a field of wildflowers.

An artful snapshot may be taken, but only if one is ready. If not, by the time you've gotten the camera out your car for a composition, the earth has moved ever so slightly, the sun has hidden behind the roof of a house and the leaves have lost their luster. He calmly sharpened the three pencils, aware of how the image of a beautiful landscape, be it visible to the physical eyes or conceptual, will dissipate more quickly from the conscious, if one tries to cling to it. The autumn colors fade and the last image impressed is a dull and gray admonishment for the person who tried to cling to a passing of some few seconds.

With his left hand he braced the top of the tablet at an angle and concentrated on the imaginary horizon of blue where it met the tops of the trees. He drew this first line across the upper portion of the page. Then, at about where the trees were rooted, he drew another line. The girl had stopped moving. She held onto a bar of the little merry go round and leaned away from it in what seemed to be a gesture of curiosity mixed with desire. There was no other child to push it around with her seated atop the small metallic disk. Under the spell of a melancholy slant of afternoon sun, the man thought he could hear a faint and subtle hint of time passing. She did not seem to be in such a mood as to try giving the wheel a push just for herself. That would have been a slow and brief turn, at any rate. She did, however, appear to want to go on a twirl and the man felt sad for her. It then seemed odd that she looked directly at him. The instant he thought that she had done so, her free hand raised upward in what may have been a wave, a friendly acknowledgment, but with a ballet like slowness the gesture continued upward and in its position above her the arm and hand floated back and forth.

He disregarded the base line, telescoped his attention to her and quickly made a preliminary sketch, using the lightest touch of the hard graphite pencil—so as not to make the first lines too dark too soon. The full view of her body, being prominent on the page, eliminated most of the environment. He did not attempt to draw the merry-go-round or the bar that she held onto, nor the ground she stood on, though he did retain his original intention of including the trees in some way. Her slightly downward pointed feet were just beginning a leap from an invisible platform of gravity, like a tree that is necessarily rooted, yet compelled to grow upward and toward the light.

She could have been a slim art-deco nymph, posed in that idealized moment of a performance where the dancer appears she might be lifted completely off the earth, her reach suspended, just as if she were about to leap away from the merry-go-round—if it were spinning. From within, however, a faint criticism of this concept. The compassionate voice of a teacher said: There is a good deal more to her depth. Sure, you have drawn her in a composed grace; her hair has the effect of a breeze and her own movement, but she is not a solo swan dance. The interior of her experience, the privacy of her being, unseen by the average theatre goer, has an undertow from which no man returns, a dynamic implication of something dangerous and deadly. That you have depicted her as peaceful is commendable. It is the affirmative aspect that a child prefers to see. But to draw her as mildly happy is not enough.

He turned the page and re-drew her as if she were on the edge of ecstatic laughter, just beginning to discover a new and insane abandon. Her hair now flew about in a storm of chaos, enflamed with life in reaction to an accost of her forward moving violence. He drew leaves with monster faces in her hair and in the air as they escaped from the threatening branches, bent, and breaking in the background. She was about to dive into an unknown, her mouth slightly open, eyes fixed. He had not yet considered that if she were a human child, as opposed to an amoral fairy, she should be dressed. When this did occur to him, he was in a predicament as to her being a spirit. What would she wear, in association with trees, other than apple blossoms? Ridiculous! That would not do for her aggressive energy.

Realistically, he thought, then he smiled—amused at the word, realistically—in reference to her possibly being a wood nymph; traditionally, she would be at least partially nude. Though out of this world, she was still human in his mind, so she needed something, but he totally rejected as completely silly, the idea of her wearing a Botticelli-like flower print dress. Determined, he politely gave her a veil of modesty. In an out of context cheating of motif, he imagined it to be an opaque orange poppy, frail and wind ripped. That it slightly covered and pressed against her was a compensation that allowed her form to be seen without being completely revealed.

It had not been his intention to imagine her merely as an incarnation of a divine being manifested into a material form, as if he were an illustrator for a Victorian story book about fairies and goblins. He did envy very much the talent of the artists who drew the scenes for George McDonald and the like and so could not resist imitating them. In the quiet of his apartment, he would stare at the fantasies in his picture books and relax into a peaceful melancholy of meditation on the dark mystery among the roots and grass and stems of an unkempt garden. What sort of entities in nature might paint the designs on the wings of butterflies or compose the notes of bird songs?

Not entirely sweet and sentimental, he also appreciated the ambiguity of the austere Lord Dunsany and others like him. The poetry of Rosette and, of course, the paintings of the Pre-Raphaelites. He liked the lively variety of the impressionists; the bright and the somber, a nostalgic country lane near a village at dusk, the strong contrasts in a Van Gogh, the watery prettiness of a Monet. On his walls were the small prints that he cut out of art magazines, in cheap frames he acquired from the secondhand store. When he did listen to music, which was not often, the brief severity of Erik Satie was nice for a while. When he was in the mood for a symphony, a pastoral by Grieg or Vaughan Williams. He would never waste his time with all the works by any composer. Most often, only one movement out of an entire repertoire was enough.

By nature, passive and quiet, he usually preferred a peaceful landscape, lots of trees with shadows, Pre-Raphaelite girls burning autumn leaves at sunset, Russian steppes, the northern renaissance domestics of Dutch interiors, British country folk in fields that looked like they could be set in a Thomas Hardy novel. He felt that he could walk into and be at home with people of a Scandinavian room where an austere sadness is composed in a tradition of silence. A stark reflection of slanted light onto a window frame is in equal partnership to the shyness in the eyes of an attractive and pensive girl.

These preludes into dark nights of soul were as pleasant for him to contemplate as the stone wall of a ruin would be to a gardener. The slightly sad expression of the young woman in a portrait would haunt him. Not that he felt compelled to figure out or research what lay behind the mystery. It was the nuance of the mystery in and of itself that intrigued him. He naturally leaned toward style over content, even if the two, as a polyphony, are what make a story interesting. Style, however, should be the dominating factor; because where there is mostly content, there is no poetry. Only the meanings in words.

He had just finished the drawing and was leaning back against the edge of the tabletop, admiring his work, when he took note of the boy. The first impression of him, standing about ten to fifteen feet to his left, was of a curious, but polite reservation, that of a child who is waiting for permission to approach and study what they perceive might be the important activity of an adult. Upon being discovered, the boy smiled. But did not speak a word. With no other communication or sign that he would approach, or even wanted to, the boy simply remained where he was, with his concentrated, yet passive and detached observance of the peculiar thing that interested. The man, struck by the solid stare, soon realized that, obviously, it was not merely the action or appearance of an eccentric artist that the boy had been studying. Feeling a little disturbed under the watchful stillness, the man suddenly imagined himself to be a large goldfish in a garden pool—being looked at by a house cat.

But of course, the fish, suspended in its cool and comfortable oblivion, would be unaware of the cat, as it sat peacefully at the pools edge and sent its desire, transformed into awareness, down past the shimmering veil, penetrating the surface from its point of view in a higher dimension. The boy, like the cat, had for some time been patiently waiting for the fish to move closer to the surface. Perhaps, the man had done just that. The cat and fish were now, in their stillness of instinct, looking at each other. The distant nature and stationary reserve on the part of the boy was not, at this moment, assumed by the man to be a human child's feeling of inferiority.

He instead realized that neither of them would be allowed to completely cross the expanse that divided them. The boy's appearance suggested that subtle elements of thought moved into and out of the thicks and thins of the universe in surprising ways. The adept and predatory of nature would be able to visit the environments of various creatures. They might float like leaves between two worlds and have the esoteric words of the insane written on them. Beings who breathed, however, and were conscious; they could only briefly dip into another realm, might visit, but never be at home.

The boy suddenly made a spontaneous turn of his head and looked away, with an aristocratic sort of indifference, toward those tall guardians that shadowed over the playground. The man naturally followed with his own line of sight and discovered the girl was no longer there. He turned back toward where the boy had been standing and he, as well, was gone. Like that change of focus that clears what was a blur, he perceived a shift of conception. Everything he experienced, what was considered real (the word that made him smile), was as much a dream, a fantasy.

"Tell me what you would like." Said the boy.

"I would like you to push me around." Said the girl.

"If I do, you have to promise to give me something."

"What would you like? My wish will be your command."

"Pay a visit to those men, in that picnic over there and listen."

"That is way too easy of a dare. Besides, I like to do that."

"Reveal yourself, then. Up close. And steal a cookie."

"I'll think about it. But tell me what you think."

"I think you look rather pretty, dressed as a flower."

She laughed. "Push me around. Push me." She said.

Then, climbing onto the merry go round, she stood.

"You better hold onto the bar if you're afraid."

"That I might fly away? And leave you? Never."

"And I can hear the very accent of your voice in the only two things you said in all that four hours' crossing: first, 'the sea-board of Demonland.' Then, an hour later, I should think, very low and dream-like. 'This is the first sip of Eternity.' "

—E. R. Eddison

Another Introduction to the Design

If we examined closely the concrete of the sidewalk of a city park we might stroll through; as well, the little pond where ducks float about and fish swim in, we would detect a frightening movement—other than the ducks and the fish. Because, deeper than any reed would dare intrude its root or fish could burrow into the mud, we (with our science of mind and technology) are able to see the evidence of a flickering substance that only seems to exist: A wonderland where patterns are the threads in the process of weaving themselves into various concentrations of mass, devising the fields of air and water and rock—whirlpools of gravities. Between these wheels and spirals and at their centers, beyond the hum of creation, we would be confronted by a stillness (what might also be called an emptiness, a silence), so vast that a mere change in the speed of the vibration in the ground might very well cause one to fall through that sidewalk.

Knowing we will eventually leave the illusory comfort of our Newtonian universe, should we not consider taking a seat on the park bench and observe the show as it unfolds before us? But of course, our inquisitive nature will inspire us to continue our sojourn, during which we might happen onto a conversation of eccentric professors on a Saturday afternoon picnic. Drawn to their odd presence, we listen to the curious debate between the good intentioned and the wizened. Spoken words, like sprouting seeds from the fallen fruit by which the inner state of a person is known, grow into conflicting and intertwining thought forms that merge and divide and spread out like a tree. We observe, in our detachment, the necessary element of chaos and imperfection, the game of chance which had so disturbed Einstein he became obsessed at finding a unified field theory to prove the creator was not dreaming, that God was not playing dice.

It is not surprising then, that for a psychological shelter, we seek security with a belief in a clockwork universe and put ourselves into it with such intensity that we become affected—crazy, like mad hatters; incoherent in the preaching of a simplistic doctrine made complicated, as if there were such a thing as permanence and a single linear thread of time that contains within it all of every ripple from every pebble cast into a pond. There is a profound reason why Jesus said one cannot know from which direction the wind of the Holy Spirit will blow. And why Hamlet said that readiness is all.

The blatant lies of our senses project a material universe and we are subject to the fear of darkness that we believe is on the other side. The assumption of a meaningless void is only a shadow cast by the body of our collective thought form. The light, which is all-pervading, is invisible and can be seen only if it is reflected by an objective universe. A desire, that we all have, to be safe and secure within a womb of peaceful predictability, is what may have compelled even an Einstein to look for a cause-and-effect creator in mathematics and C. S. Lewis to attempt an argument for the doctrine of predestination in his up-side-down metaphysical horror story, The Great Divorce. The dichotomies and paradox (that we are all uncomfortable with for more than a few minutes) that are found in any one of the cosmologies of science and religion, may still be used as a launch for a dive down into the rabbit hole, if we are brave enough. Or, simply curious, like children.

Though we may be fearful at the prospect of discovering there is no solid blanket protecting one from the bogeyman hiding under the bed, we will be at least entertained at the surreal quality of our half dream when we peek through an opening and see how the moonlight illumines our imagination. We will be thankful for an unusual cast of characters—scary and nonsensical as their stories are. A problem arises, however, when individuals invest their entire intellect in acquiring grains of material and filling up their bins of short lives, all of which are only fleeting expressions of the Spirit as it moves upon the face of the waters. Knowing that the manifested thought form's claims to physical existence are insubstantial as the waves on an ocean, Yogananda advised us to not "… get caught in the machine of the world. It is too exacting. By the time you get what you are seeking, your nerves are gone. The heart is damaged." He also said. "By evading self-analysis, people go on being robots, conditioned by their environment."

Without the transcendence found in knowledge of the self, work is a lifeless, repetitive prison of sameness that re-enforces hypnotic attachment to the mechanisms built for slavery. Tired and defeated, people just go along to get along and before they realize it, they have become either Morlocks or Eloi. They have lost the ability to even contemplate the existence of a free-will. The spirit of independence and individual liberty is incrementally eaten away by a welfare state that takes away the choices and the will to choose, which makes it easier for unconstitutional mandates to be implemented and enforced. School boards, teachers' unions, and city councils, having become infested by the weeds of mind control, are able to use guilt and fear-porn to boss people into compliance—educating their children into hateful little devils. Compare the cultural revolution of China with the contemporary shaming tactics of the so called Woke of contemporary America. Blind and angry sleep walking dead—opposite to what the word, woke, originally means.

Examples of hypocrisy abound. The undercurrent of doublethink, being a dumbed down language of slogans, should be obvious: Haters of conservatives referring to conservatives as haters. Meanings are twisted. A common sense understanding of nuance is completely lost. During the Civil War, the uniforms worn by the Union Army of the Republican President, Abraham Lincoln, were blue. Yet, today, so called Republican states are referred to as red, the color that Russian and Chinese Communists used for representing themselves. The Democrat party (the party of the Confederacy and the Ku Klux Klan) is now referred to as blue. These recent twisting and confusing associations in meaning are intentional. If an illiterate thief can plan to break into a building, so to an egotistical elitist ideologue into the institutions of media.

For instance, a manipulator will use words with positive connotations (like love), while committing a cruelty. This has the purpose of defeating the victim by way of creating a mental chaos. Much like the tactic used by the drug addicted abuser of a spouse, in which the naïve and confused partner or family member (sometimes a friend), is made to feel both guilty and angry. The clever dominant member of the co-dependency will then by-pass the act of remorse and simply use an innuendo followed by silence, inducing a self-hatred in their unaware victim. Falsely accusing the innocent person of racism (critical race theory), the Communists and Corporate Fascists, conscious in their use of this tactic, are deserving of the deepest circle of Hell, because they knowingly betray the Living Spirit.

The term, miss-information, will be twisted and invoked as an excuse for dis-regarding any discussion that questions the leftist agenda. To unperson with labels (insulting and calling them names) is a nonsensical, seemingly simplistic, but ingeniously passive aggressive way to murder reason and burn down the structures of civilization. With a mentality of rapists who leap from a dark alley, the evil flies out of their mouths in a coward's method of hit and run. A blatant characteristic of mechanical newspeak. Watch the life-like mannequins of the main-stream media on television and you enter the twilight zone.

To see the horror behind the façade requires a spiritual knowledge—acquired through self-inquiry. A degree in philosophy, religion, or psychology will not suffice. For the university educated Leftist Americans to be so ignorant as to call themselves Communist is just simply bizarre. Very often they have been children, Che Guevara t-shirt wearing white liberal racist trust fund caste system elitists, condescending with good deed preaching of welfare equity toward those they consider under-privileged (those below them, the underlings: The workers). They call religion the opiate of the masses; themselves being dull-witted converts to a religion of imperial central government. With lies and fictional twisting of history by the varieties of critical theory propaganda, they are innocently recruited as informers on those who do not concede to their doctrine.

With little or no conscious intention, their individuality is absorbed into the mob mind. But unlike the Borg of Star Trek or the alien children in Village of the Damned, the I-phone connected hive of thought police becomes invisible, a multi-faceted and quickly evolving mass behavior with no evident leader or cell. Instructions for movement are inserted by a cohort of cooperative and competitive organizations into the mental process of normal looking humans. Just as consumers are advertised to by different companies that use the same Pavlov technique, so are the useful idiots for the ambiguous revolution controlled by the vampiric thought forms (popularly known as devils) that will eventually drag them down into Socialist Hell.

Do-gooders (primarily undergrads) who do not have the wisdom of true compassion in sacrifice, are enlisted into an army in service to an organic declaration of war on reason, themselves confused into a state of vulnerability. The method is a mix of emotions and pseudo-logic: Complicated philosophy that flatters the reader with simple and easy to absorb slogans, seducing them into believing they are superior and therefor have the right to commit violence. To the thuggish criminal mind, justice becomes associated with revenge against the accused oppressor.

Like the lab rat persistently pawing at a lever that no longer supplies the cheese, there is a pleasure of self-reinforcement for the conscious that has been taken over by a demon. The destruction and murder brought about by the revolution will be thought of as a bringing of mercy to the oppressed by eliminating the oppressor and therefor revenge is mercy. The insane pseudo-logic of this method is intended to bring chaos. If allowed to continue, the entire country will be beaten into poverty, except for the elite, who, remember, think of themselves as the smart ones who should be in control. All traditional institutions will be abolished. Experienced first responders, educated veterans, replaced with obedient wimps.

The revolutionist is too stupid to realize the absurdity of setting fire to an entire institution and uses a convoluted Marxist justification of "building back better" as an excuse for a self-aggrandizing indulgence and cruelty. How do you suppose the priests of the Inquisition, who condemned those of heresy to be burned alive at the stake, could live with themselves? It was because they believed with their whole hearts that what they were doing was the will of their god and that suffering would bring the so-called heretics to a humility of confession and therefor salvation.

The volunteer civilian police (weak minded adults and children with un-developed brains) who use their I-phones to spy, inform on whoever they deem to be counter-revolutionary enemies of the people (witches), are as disgusting as an illiterate medieval gossip who reports on their neighbor as having been heard speaking heresy. It bears repeating, that in the French Revolution, after the ruling class had their heads chopped off, it was those accused of being anti-revolutionary who were next in line to have their necks laid down under the blade. Many of those executed had originally been revolutionists themselves. The suppression of individual consciousness is a reign of terror that appeals to fear and the selfish desire for superiority. It is how federal agents in unison with privet security companies enlist the volunteer piglets who root their snouts into their I-phones to serve the facial recognition software and computerized spy systems.

Beaten into stupidity by propaganda, the information gatherers and censors think they are serving the greater good. Their slavery to an emotional religion is the same as those who designed and built the guillotine. The control does not come from merely a central government. It comes from something more frightening, because it is ambiguous: A cancel culture that metaphorically sets fire to books and people. The current mob mind insanity, like a mutated species, is ravenous to lay waste the institutions of check and balance. In the aftermath of a civil war that is manipulated into being merely a reign of terror, the new central government will claim to bring peace and order: War is peace. We all know the name of the dictator who came after Robespierre. Order will be brought back, so that war may continue more effectively. The resulting culture will not, however, be so colorfully romantic, as it was with Wordsworth, Shelly, Coleridge, Blake, and Byron. Not, if the universities, enforcing politically correct word lists, have their way.

I, myself, would be happy, knowing that the revolutionists will eventually start eating their own, but I also know they will continue their abuse of the language, devising perversions of the rule of law, as a pretense for bringing Utopia by way of the fascist boot. If you think Federal departments given bureaucratic power to levy fines was bad, wait until you experience the newly reformed imperialist police department. Robots in human bodies will replace the strong individualists who were pushed out of their employment by the irrational defunding and the mandates of the medical establishment.

A brazen dis-regard of the Bill of Rights is a form of insurrection against the check and balance system of the Republic. There is no legislated law that demands every employee must be vaccinated or lose their job. Or that one may not go to a church, gather in a park or in their own house, enter an outdoor mall unless they have a mask on or can show documentation (their vaccination passport papers), forcing employees into playing the role of informers to the gestapo. It is disturbing that people are compliant and fearful, unable to name the mandates for what they obviously are.

Fear prevents them from being honest, with even a sense of humor. Censorship by the media, civilian informers, ideological prosecutors and judges, self-serving federal departments, the consolidating of information by a politicized spy agency, and enforcement by a thuggish political party, along with militarized police—the culmination of which is, even now, that psychological boot on the face of humanity. Currently, in Australia, all personal travel is watched and controlled through an algorithm. The individual must report regularly through their I-phone. Remember to wear the overcoat that has the star of David sewn on if you go out to the grocery store. And be sure to have your papers on you in case you are stopped and asked to present them to the officer wearing the swastika armband.

Because children are not currently educated in history and do not have fully developed brains, they are more easily and quickly manipulated than are adults. The opening chapter on revolution begins with students, always the first to participate in book burning, as in Nazi Germany and Communist China. A riot of Animal Farm Red Guard spy pigs, bored teenagers not allowed to go to class and participate in sports, the unemployed aftermath of an unnecessary shut down of the economy in response to an oddly well timed epidemic. When schools and universities do go back into session, children are ordered to wear worthless masks (the real purpose of which is to psychologically smother).

Then, they are taught an ideological perversion of science, politically correct literature, and propaganda. The study of civics is replaced with shallow sociological race theories on the level of cartoon manga heroes—creating spoiled brats who imagine themselves to be freedom fighters. Doomed to repeat the history they have not learned, turned into slogan chanting thugs, tools who burn buildings; while their comrade teachers, administrators, unions, and federal department over-seers commit cultural genocide by throwing entire segments of western civilization into the memory hole of generational forgetfulness. When was the last time you saw a poster that quoted the words of Martin Luther King?

Not knowing who they really are or what they really think, they seek to make anyone who disagrees with them into a non-person—to be destroyed, a monument defaced, an image scraped off the wall. The vandals are Russian Communists who imprisoned entire villages in concentration work camps. They are the students of the Chinese Cultural Revolution who dragged their teachers and old people out into the street, beat, humiliated, and sometimes tortured them to death. They are the German Nazis. They are the Socialist Democrat New Hitler Youth of America who, in their naivete, supported the Manchurian Candidate administrations that betrayed our allies in Iraq and Afghanistan—leaving the women of those countries to be humiliated, beaten, raped, and murdered by the Taliban. They are the dead souls who sold out to Satan, then proceeded to hand America over to the United Nations of a Byzantine World Government for the sake of a political ideology that is akin to an Islamist hatred for individual liberty, a Mussolini Fascist partnership with corporate industry and Communist China: Work camps for Nike and consumers for Hollywood.

They are all (even grown men and women) like little teen-age girls with I-phone cameras, feeling themselves up as powerful documentarian Spielbergs, warriors for the double speak of return to normalcy as servitude to the state. The Attorney General (associated with a company that makes money teaching critical race theory in schools), in cohort with White House political staff and the National School Board Association, uses his agency to investigate parents as being domestic terrorists, because they oppose the Marxist school boards advocacy of Critical Race Theory. Normalcy is state service without resistance: If you are against the Climate Change scam, getting an experimental shot, face mask fiascos, and vaccine passports, then you are insulted as anti-science, anti-revolutionary, suspect of being mentally ill (an enemy of the people), a domestic terrorist.

If one is feeling overwhelmed, remember that the most effective weapon against the devil is scorn. Those next-door neighbors and fellow students, even family members, recruited into being civilian thought-police; they should be laughed at, ridiculed for using their virtue posing as bumper sticker slogan concepts—one of the stupidest saying that Jesus was a Socialist. The betrayer, Judas, was the Socialist. Read John 12: 1-8. Better yet, see into the story about the coin found in the mouth of a fish. Matthew 17: 24-27. Jesus may or may not have been saying that a person should be a good citizen and pay their taxes. What is far more important is the miracle of the coin being found as Jesus directed. The message is that material (Caesar, the fish, the coin) is impermanent, created by and subject to spirit. Render that which essentially does not exist unto that which does not exist.

A failure to study scripture is also the cause of the self-righteous miss-use of the word, justice—the spiritual meaning of which they have no comprehension. If, on the other hand, those childish athletes who insulted the sacrifice of police and soldiers by turning their backs on the American flag, had bothered to cultivate even a cursory meta-physics, they would have discovered that not being perfect in wisdom, they might not want to be so preachy about Justice—seeing that judgment is a two-edged sword. Read Mathew 7:1-3. Far better to be grateful for the mercy of the Spiritual sacrifice (symbolized by Christ: Compassion, acquired only through wisdom) of a Creator.

Regardless of one's philosophical leaning (be it dualistic or non-dual), if we admit that we are, at the very least, in the world, though not of it, we can also assume that we are individuals with a free will and are saved by the forgiveness at the pinnacle of the crucifixion, without which, we (not having the omniscience of the all-pervading creator), would inevitably plummet into self-destruction. Try explaining this to a Leftist. Unfortunately, it seems the frontal lobes of the obedient to slogans appear to be in the thirteen to nineteen-year-old developmental stage of idiocy.

Mistaking their emotions of sympathy for virtue, the children virtue-signal their quasi-intellectual activism, considering themselves to be hipsters who are in on what they have been convinced will be the altruistic state that will come after the revolution. Incapable of any logic at all, the minimum of which would bring them into an awareness of their innate intelligence, they would be horrified at discovering their souls have been transformed into insects, a swarm that riots as a system of blood demons—spoiled, angry, giddy from their satanic war dance of low-level vibrations into acts of obscene cruelty—oblivious as drug addicts.

Their insane cackle of summer vacation laughter would be amusing were it not that the murder of reason might very well contribute to a coming decade of suffering and the possible death of the only nation in the world that was founded on the Biblical concept of equality. The sacrifice of those who gave their lives (the Union Army of the Civil War, the American Military of World War II, Draftees of the War in Viet-Nam, the Volunteers in Iraq and Afghanistan) is dismissed, if not openly insulted, for a bacchanal on the periphery of rampage and meaningless bloodshed (safely, to be sure, knowing they have their parent's homes and dorm rooms to return to) after dancing with devils in the anarchy of the streets during the fake election of 2020.

These are the descendants of the Marxist political philosophers who were chased out of Germany by the Nazis. Take note that Fascists and Communists historically have been in the habit of deadly competition. Research the Spanish Civil War and the converging of ulterior motives that preceded it. Look at the political science mixed with manipulative techniques of psychology. Many of those European coffee shop revolutionaries ended up at Colombia University in the 1930's, infiltrating their methods of propaganda into the entire public school system. Their professional students, who went on to become teachers themselves, programed with cyborg software to continue inserting the seeds of evil into the following generation. Those who are conscious of what they are doing are most certainly Satanic. They would have to be, to brazenly contradict the deeply life affirming and spiritually inspired founding of The United States. Thinking themselves to be the aristocrats of smartness, they have replaced common sense with complicated sociological race theories aimed at dividing people into conflict. Ruled entirely by their egos, in their delusion of success at the manipulation of the minds of children, the academics believe that they are now the controllers.

They are, ironically, the bottom feeders of the corporate/government pyramid scheme. Besides the medical establishment and other politically adept, it is the untouchable (members of the military industrial complex) and the cleverly anonymous, very, very rich organized crime syndicates and their deep state comrades who will pick up the pieces after the war has brought down all the buildings of the Republic. They will manipulate a tired and beaten human race by twisting logic as easily as the Devil will quote scripture. The pretense of a utopia will be designed by the smirking demon possessed and by the members of the one-party government who think as one. The make-work will be carried out by an anthill of technocrats. A brave new world order will then be built. And be sure, it will be a fascist state. At the university, where creative inquiry and the liberal arts have been corrupted into indoctrination, any debate in political philosophy will be as pointless as bringing a lawsuit against a devil to a court run by devils.

The political philosophers (scholarly and otherwise), thinking they will be the ones in charge, are very much like Doctor Faustus, the alchemist wizard who used magic and sold his soul to gain the world, then, in the tragic version, lost it all in the end. Once they have served their purpose as propagandists, they will be eliminated by those little inquisitors who were once their students. Even now, they have become the teacher's union, schoolboard members, health departments, city councils: Dead souls who sit with smug indifference and politburo expressions. As for the professors, who signed their names in blood and created the little Frankenstein monsters, like their literary ancestor, they will forever be damned into an eternal destruction at the event horizon of a black hole that was once the heart of an Archangel.

Marxism is a philosophical and nicely sterilized word that is available for arm-chair revolutionaries who can then avoid reference to their embarrassing murderous comrades: Bolsheviks, Khmer Rouge, Shining Path. Their text-book Utopias are a complicated labyrinth wherein there lives a Minotaur that will devour the soul of the lost undergrad. The architecture of this impressive temple to the god of a ruthless government is meant to distract. It contains intersecting hallways to empty rooms, stairways to basements and isolated attics—layers of cross-referenced logic—the rhetoric by which a self-deluded intellectual would use to argue with an angel who is attempting to save the mortal from sinking deeper into Hell. The useful idiots, digging of their own graves, are motivated by an egotistical elitism—in that Communism really would work if the smart people, like themselves, were in charge.

In a speech ironically given at the leftist bastion of Harvard, Solzhenitsyn warned the United States of the incremental corruption: The greed of immoral Capitalists who at present are betraying the United States—eventually selling out to the Communists in China. He warned that the enemy, imbedding themselves into federal bureaucracies, would have the power to manipulate (propagandize, censor) through the media (the thought police) and erode the first amendment. Cancel culture would make people afraid to speak. And so, considering themselves virtuous and above the law, in the smokescreen of confusion, the fraudulent election was orchestrated.

Whatever name is taken (Socialists, Progressives, or any sheep's clothing disguise), they gain power through the media to entertain and enter the minds of children with a bread and circus propaganda that is meant to intimidate through humiliation. In school, if a child does not play along with the indoctrination, an insulting accusation by way of innuendo (racist, sexist, homophobe) is implied by a false narrative. Smothered by a blanket condemnation (the silent threat of being ostracized or outright name calling), the child is incrementally beaten into submission. As experts in psychology, Communists know how to use a base emotion re-enforcing drug: The illusion of empowerment through a self-righteous hatred for those labeled as the enemy. The resulting cancel culture has made people afraid to speak. Taking advantage of the confusion, anything can be orchestrated under the smokescreen of a false accusation, sometimes communicated with just a silent murder in the eyes. It is true that the innocent and hardworking who were asleep could not have seen the evil seeds that were planted in the night. Silently, the little newspeaks were integrated into the language. There came the changing of the definitions of words to mean the opposite of their original use. In a certain collegiate dictionary, the entry for Fascist was changed from the activity of far leftists to those of the far right. Little by little, traditional meanings are destroyed by extreme contradictory definitions.

There has been a dumbing down of the reading material in school and public libraries. One might say, in many cities, there are no such things as public libraries. Their interiors have become sterile, with employees hiding behind plastic partitions, pathetically obedient patrons condescended to by teen-age volunteer mask police, dictator department heads making sure that all arbitrary mandates are obeyed, formerly nice middle-aged ladies now angrily ordering people to stand six feet apart. The pandemic gave permission for all the little dictators to come out their closets. School and public library administrators, who receive taxpayer funding, for decades, have secretly used the money to make deals with small press companies, telling them that they will buy large numbers of books from them if they disguise their radical leftist propaganda as graphic novels for children. They have been in the process of turning the library into a community center for incremental socialism—experimenting on children. It is the atmosphere of a low-budget 1950's science fiction movie set. It is not a library.

Anything with a nuance that does not conform to the progressive agenda is either removed or kept in the minutest number. An apologetic biography of Lenin is put on prominent display. Copies of the two or three very thin ghost written auto-biographies of Obama are a plenty. The encyclopedic writings of Winston Churchill are not to be found. A person is hard pressed to find even one conservative periodical on the magazine rack. True, my experience may be a personal observation from the outside—not being a member of the library board. I admit to having the bias of a childhood spent in the quiet mystical atmosphere of a large soft-lit room surrounded by books.

The propagandists, until recently, have relied on a method of omission combined with political correctness. Real, factual news goes un-reported. Lies are told, over and over, until they are believed. Try to get a reading list from your local schoolboard. When you finally do, count the missing authors and books you consider essential world literature that are not there, having metaphorically met the fate of Fahrenheit 451. The icons of American culture are taken out of context and are banned for incorrectness. I would not be critical of the setting aside of "Huckleberry Finn", if it were replaced by any two or three of Mark Twain's short stories that show a profound love and compassion for black people of his time. He even wrote a positive portrayal of a tough cowgirl, admittedly with a detached satire, but with an intelligence and sense of humor that essentially invented stand-up comedy. Maybe it is because they refuse to read great literature or when they try to do so, they interpret with extreme prejudice. It seems leftists are too stupid to understand the nuance of time and place—especially their own.

Many works do need to be relegated to the dusty shelves of the museum basement, which happens through a natural evolutionary change in culture and a mature embarrassment at past insensitivity. An example being the use of Caucasian actors, ruining what otherwise would have been an epic masterpiece, in portraying Chinese peasants in the film version of "The Good Earth." The hateful attempted destruction, however, of an artist and their entire collection of work is shocking. Laura Ingalls Wilder, the author of "Little House on the Prairie", was unjustly treated when politically correct busy bodies had her name removed from a literary organization, simply because one of her characters briefly spoke (as a character) about Indians in context of that specific time and place. Snobbish elitists continually condemn out of context.

Another example of Leftist idiocy was when the name of the famous brain surgeon, Ben Carson (who happens to be conservative) was removed from a school of medicine and replaced with the name of a performer who had nothing to do with medical research or education. Cultural bigots, like Muslims who destroy Buddhist statues, or Protestants who violated cathedrals, seek to destroy the souls of people. They will throw the photographs of your parents into a dumpster fire. They will keep you in prison until you sign the document that condemns what you believe in.

Political prisoners are de-moralized with torture for the purpose of taking away their humanity. A recent example of humiliating insult to psychologically imprisoned Americans is the defacing and destruction of monuments. Rioters attempted to remove the statue of Thomas Jefferson, apparently because he owned slaves at a time when slave ownership was common in the world. It was so in all cultures through-out all of history and is still practiced by black Muslims in Africa, the Taliban in Iraq and Afghanistan, and the Communists in China. Again, the purpose of the attempt to topple the statue was not merely to condemn Jefferson's failure to eradicate slavery within his environment. The purpose was to destroy a culture. Not that rioters are necessarily conscious of the devils driving them.

More like drunken peasants, too ignorant to understand the refinements of truth in the words of Martin Luther's Reformation or the beauty of light reflected in the pictures on stained-glass windows—rampaging into the cathedrals, they broke, pillaged, and burned.

Consider whether the self-righteous white liberal do-gooders would be so arrogant as to tell a black Christian church they should stop reading the Psalms, because King David owned slaves. The Old Testament hero also, by the way, was guilty of murder, had civilians tortured and kidnapped women. Adultery with Bathsheba was the least of his sins. One might say the best—considering it brought about the conception of Solomon, making David the ancestor to Mary, the mother of Jesus. Ironic as that may be (a debate on the dichotomy of a God who goes on walks with Satin in the garden, later), it also just so happens there is a notion in the Bible which implies that someone (as contemptible as King David and later, Saul of Tarsus) can be transformed through an assault by the Holy Ghost, faith, confession, and forgiveness. Our greatest heroes have been guilty of the greatest crimes. Who shall cast the first stone?

Note: (Answer: The instrument of Karma, I suppose). But, Karma, as an aspect of Samsara, is infinite. That means, of course, you cannot pay back what you owe. You will forever be in the cycle of birth, suffering, death, and re-birth. As far as I can see, there are two ways out of this dilemma: 1. The path of Faith. Give oneself completely up unto the Christ. Or, 2. The path of knowledge. Advaita Vedanta (not two). In respect to the transcendence of Devotion and Yoga, I am open, but my Protestant individuality is impatient with tiresome ritual and very suspicious of Priests and Gurus.

Socialists (especially Pope Judas) belong to a variety of cults with leaders and spokesmen. Atheists, as well. Doctrines (some good, some evil) are in all denominations of politics. They are professed by philosophies as much as they are preached by religions. The primary opposing difference between Communism and Capitalism is that Capitalism requires freedom for the individual. The Bill of Rights is the doctrine. Contrasting, the extreme danger to this freedom is the atheistic science of psychology mixed with political philosophy. The subtle methods of mind control by Communist sympathizers (you may call them Mussolini Fascists if you like, corporate/government oligarchs) are currently leavened into all our institutions: government, learning—the Big Brother of them all being the news organizations, which Malcolm X referred to as all powerful media. At present, that would include algorithmically ambiguous social platforms.

The manipulations by perversions of logic are a direct result of the denial of Spirit. A smartly polished intellect, under the spell of the ego, will conjure up the most horrendous construct, simply for the purpose of destruction. Example: Queer Theory (an extreme Freudian sexualizing of children) is promoted by academics as an excuse for grooming grade school children into questioning their sexual identity. This is coupled with Critical Race Theory. The reason they do this is to make children hate themselves and the culture they come from, divide children from their parents. Then, replace the children's spiritual freedom that they inherited (rights that are endowed by a creator) with a new and strictly materialist culture of mere human rights—given to them (to be taken away) by a human government (Communist). Revolution.

As we try our best to ignore the lies and arrogance of leftist controlled media (for the sake of our mental health, if not our souls) and as we persevere in our own research, we best think on what is lovely, true, and just. Our study, however, should not be a total retirement, a retreat from battle. Replenishing as prayer and meditation is, a pleasant hermit's solitude of recluse is not allowed for long. Krishna implied as much to Arjune when he admonished the Prince to arise as a warrior from his excuse of grief and his attempt to run from duty. This desire to escape from the game of creation is problematic—to say the least, as difficult as trying to get out of bringing pay back to the murderer of one's lover. The opera is not over until the Diva has put a knife into the evil Baron, sung her last aria and leaps to her death. Or, to say it not quite so melodramatically: The brave Hobbit, Sam, must rescue the ring bearer, Frodo, from the Tower of Cirith Ungol and help his friend up that grim mountain, that he may brave the Cracks of Doom for the cast of the ring into the fiery pit.

Meanwhile, down below, worshipers of the material (like what Moses may have seen when he descended from Mount Sinai) continue to allow their base emotions to be agitated into a mass psychosis by the egotistical technocrats of media. That would be Amazon, Facebook, Twitter, Google, Microsoft, the drug companies, and governmental medical establishment—which is an entity that includes Bill Gates and his comrade, Fauci, the Nazi Doctor who advocates experimentation on children through the mandate of masks and injecting them with a gene therapy drug. Obedient to the low-level vibrations of Satanic manipulation, the mentally abused masses follow the instructions of the rulers in white coats.

When the State benevolently gives you permission to go to church, you must not sing. You must not congregate after the service, as you usually would, for mutual support. You may not hold hands or lay them on each other in expressions of healing. But rather, you must separate with social distance from each other. Be isolated like lab rats in behavior modification experiments. Wear the mask as a symbol of silencing communication. Get vaccinated as a symbol of submission to the corporate medical complex, Line up for the train that will take you to the re-education camp.

Business as usual. Lots of money to be made selling drugs, telling lies to re-enforce fear. But be sure you do not offend the big boss: (Mussolini government/corporate crony Fascist—fill in the blank, etcetera, etcetera, etcetera). They did not get where they are by being nice guys. So, it is prudent to not let the neighborhood criminal know that you are the one who called the cops on him. He knows where you park your car. If you are caught criticizing Stalin in your letter to a friend or family member, you will be sent to Siberia. Communicate an opinion opposing the agenda, the thought police will be on you.

Even if you are not the sort to risk being burned alive at the stake or hacked to death by an insane Islamist; let's say you are not a conservative activist, artist with a conscience or translator of the Bible out of Latin into English. You just want to keep your friends, have a sit around after turkey dinner, watch a football game on holiday with extended family, keep peace with your fellow corporate-ladder climbing bureaucrats— sorry, you will fall with them. Even if you are not like them, duped as they are, builders of the Tower of Babel, greedy or simply bludgeoned by fear into ignorance. It would be better if you shook off the dust from your sandals—now. To remain in a state of sin that is a bearing of false witness to yourself, is to feed a demon that will eventually explode and destroy you.

The ignorant are pathetic, but forgivable. Far more horrifying is the state of those devils who know the truth and yet work energetically toward the destruction of individual liberty, who smirk at you when you expose their vile affront; they (ruthless as the Spanish Inquisitors) are never admonished, have no guilt, and actively attempt to replace the Spirit with material (reach Heaven by way of a tall stack of bricks). It is an apt metaphor to describe the nature of a uniformed society that will ultimately self-destruct—radical sameness being in direct opposition to the diversity of life. More so, for its fractal growth into a complicated machine.

Computers crash. A self-driving car swerves into a tree, the batteries explode, the occupants are melted, and it takes an entire day to put out the fire. What if the internet were to collapse, like the tower? How long would a recovery take? A fall back into the nineteen-hundreds is the image very often depicted. A Victorian feudalistic steam punk anarchy would rule the world. Then again, if it is true that the A-I system is irretrievably imbedded, it would be unlikely for it to lose its' influence over the world economy. It is probable that it will simply adapt (like the Roman Empire into the Holy Roman Bank, or Mafia, if your will) and grow stronger. A self-preserving fail-safe system will have already been programmed for a complete take over mode. Any major crisis, or the anticipation of it, is usually reacted to with an irrational fear, re-enforced and manipulated by those who know how to use a crisis to their own advantage. A desperation will allow for mercenary forces to infiltrate deeper into the ruling hierarchy of the city that has become over-dependent on what was originally a servant. Read Machiavelli.

The methods of propaganda and control, as depicted in 1984, have slipped in rather surreptitiously. Even those who saw it coming and who tried to stop it within the system were either absorbed or canceled out by a corrupted media. In a truly Byzantine type of intrigue (like as in a spy novel), the head of Interpol is suddenly disappeared just when the Chinese Communists have gained access into the organization. When are such incidents reported and for how long? Don't bother looking for justice. You will wander the hallways of bureaucrat Hell forever. Welcome to Kafka's Castle. Seeking escape, you might hope the end is near. Maybe the Kingdom of God is at hand—in this timeline, at any rate.

I am told, however, that the kingdom is eternal, in the moment and there is only an end to the dream, from which we will awake, have a good laugh about, then fall asleep again for another adventure. In the context of this play, that we are either watching or performing in, until the final curtain comes down on our tragedy (some say a comedy of errors), we will suspend our dis-belief. While in Plato's cave of a movie house, watching the previews of coming attractions (entertainments to scare hell out you), we will be enticed with sex and provided with monsters of violence. The world government (personified in film as that mad scientist) is our horror story in two parts.

Part one: The computer (2001, A Space Odyssey) takes over and we all become the slave to a machine. How many times have you seen a human blithely trotting along, half blindly on that Newtonian sidewalk, staring at an I-phone, scrolling through inane twitter feeds, or following its directions to that restaurant they were looking for? They are like dumb animals being led around by robots, incapable of inter-action with all the sensory universe around them. This is rather sad, at the very least, but also dangerous. A dependency will give power to the servant. Beware of the autopilot that completely shuts out human involvement in its operation. If there is a major error, that plane is going down.

Part two: There is a war between thinking machines and humanity (the prequels to Dune) where-in there will be one of three outcomes. All of humanity will be terminated—if it has not already been absorbed into the A-I. Second, humans might be kept around as pets, like the kid at the grocery store who fixes the self-checkout register just before you are about to slam your fist into it. Even computers need some human involvement, minimal as it may seem to be. The third possible result of the war is that humans prevail and take a hard stand against the robots—even while they keep them around. Humans do love their toys. And Power.

The environment of the machine is well depicted by that fable of a King who tried to build a tower to Heaven—symbolic of the pride of educated ignorance, such as the scientist: Doctor Frankenstein, mesmerized into believing life is material (solid), pieced together and animated by a cause-and-effect physical force, such as electricity. Whether Mary Shelly was able to acknowledge the spiritual, I don't know, and I really don't care. I found her novel too lugubrious and clever in its academic style of intellectual show-off to wade all the way through. Yes, I am sure it would have been a success for its profound insight, even if her husband had not improved its narrative. Only Kubrick's HAL, the computer, is a monster of equal status. In fact, HAL is a manifestation of evil that surpasses even Mary Shelly's invention, because unlike the human monster, the computer is completely lifeless.

Simply put, the philosophical materialism and magic (under a pretense of science) is a denial of the Holy Spirit (the living God), who comes and goes in ways we cannot predict or comprehend. In ignorance and dis-regard of the necessary game of competitive cooperation required for life, the power-addicted intellectual elite, and their technocrat peons, who serve the Mammon god of the state (federal grants), will sacrifice their souls. When the biology of genetics is combined with A-I mechanics, the grotesques will step out from the movie screen and be among us. By the time they are recognized for the monsters of death, that they really are, it will be too late. The human DNA will be inside the concentration camp.

The complexity, such as in free market Capitalism, inspired by the competitive nature of living beings, is what provides an evolution, an on-going-ness. The natural evolution is disturbed, however, by the inflicting of a radical uniformity. A fascist sort of mass production will sterilize and kill a species by forcing it to re-produce into a sameness. The perfectly matched bricks in a featureless wall is an apt symbol for governmental control. In response to the smothering imprisonment, I fully expect the self-defense of the life force to react like a wounded, cornered animal. Our beautiful orchestra of larks and sparrows, the landscape of garden flowers and trees, the damselfly fairies flitting about among the cattails along the shoreline, all this will retreat into hiding when the female Deity transforms into the berserker wrath of a mother protecting her children.

The on-going and evolving movement of life depends on diversity. The violent destruction of the Tower of Babel and the scattering of people into a multitude of languages and nations is the necessary action by an intelligence that promotes life. It was not a punishment, but a saving of the people from themselves. The many languages that result from the destruction of the Tower of Babel is a good thing, painful as the conflicts that result may be. As to when exactly the collapse will happen, is a guess. At present, the nuclear warheads remain in their silos. Will it be a human who pushes the button? Or will it be a computer error?

The 5-G towers are all in place. HAL is watching from every street corner. Facial recognition software follows your movements from store to store, office building and hotel lobby, hallways and from behind the screens of your computers (that you may still quaintly call televisions). There will be a war. How it plays out can be easily predicted if one reads their Abrahamic scripture and science fiction. Seeing into the future, however, is dangerous. It is not recommended, for practical reasons. For one, the seer is very often accused of being a witch who caused the sun to be eclipsed by the moon. We all know what happens to people who speak truth. They are eventually admired, long after they have been burned at the stake. Another reason is that whatever crystal ball is used, the vision could very well be that of a timeline in an alternate universe. Therefore, incorrect.

Looking at the reality in our own immediate environment, considering the frightening possibilities, what is one to do when standing on that corner (Hal's unblinking eye staring), while in wait for the light to change or for the arrival of that celestial omnibus of the mind? What if we have missed the last number seven that was on route to a higher realm? Will the ground quake open suddenly and swallow us? Should we be seriously contemplating the meta-physical quality of our state of being? Or should we just go on pretending and not worry about the course of a universe we think we have no power over?

I hope to find a nice place to sit, in a park, that is high up on a celestial hill, far enough away from the construction site of the world government, so as not to be in danger of getting hit by the falling debris while I watch the towers of artificial (fake) intelligence come tumbling down. They all come tumbling down, don't they! The great cities of all ancient civilizations. The temple of Jerusalem, Persepolis, Babylon, Alexandria, the Acropolis of Athens. The pyramids though, as monuments, do have a longevity. But so does the coliseum of Rome. The thought forms that built them, however, have long passed away. Yet, some of those demons do have a staying power. They would be the gods who inspire the icons of materialism. And in some cases (such as with those long ago sacrificial alters on the pyramids of Central America, as well the furnace of Moloch), the children in our present civilization are also prepared by their propagandists for sacrifice to the collective of Communism.

So, as one watches, or fights against the machine (for which the human life blood of individuality in humans is being bled as their minds are numbed by doublethink and hearts are ripped out by the betrayal of those they trusted), perhaps the best thing a person can do is to continue their study of the enlightened and follow the mystic's advice and their example. After all, as I imagine Marcus Aurelius might say, it is work through the spirit within ourselves that all enlightened teachers admonish us toward. Self-inquiry might be all that is required of a person—at least until we are called upon to stand up.

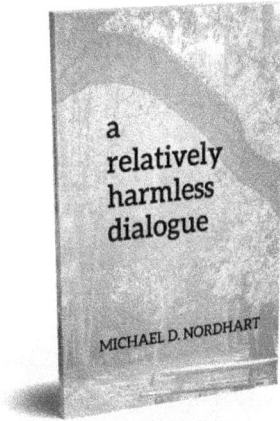

a
relatively
harmless
dialogue

MICHAEL D. NORDHART

A visit to the accompanying novel
A Relatively Harmless Dialogue

Consider a conversational debate among some students and their eccentric professors, that takes place in an atmosphere where one may feel the spirit has led you through a doorway into another dimension. It seems to be your world, yet somehow different.

In Hindu cosmology the tree grows upside down, with roots in Heaven and the branches toward the World. In Dante's Divine Comedy, Paradise is inverted and the poet flies effortlessly (falls) into the sky toward the light. The mere descriptive does not do justice to these inspired metaphysics. That is why we tell stories. The narrator in The Great Divorce, for instance, after having had a dream in which he paid a visit to Heaven by way of a bus, wakes up in abject terror. He does not fear the night he has returned to. He fears he will be a ghost when the sun rises.